GW00381325

It's A

"MAN THING!"

An easy to carry handbook of biblical directives for men

Reverend R C Francis

Published by
BTM Life Light (UK)

Copyright © 2014
Rupert C and M J Francis

All rights reserved. Written permission must be secured from the publisher to use or reproduce any part of this booklet except for use in prayer time or discussion.

Published in the United Kingdom by BTM Life Light. Unless otherwise indicated, all scripture quotations are taken from the King James Version of the Bible.

Scripture quotations noted NIV are taken from the Holy Bible NEW INTERNATIONAL VERSION

Copyright © 1973, 1984, by

The International Bible Society. Used by permission.

Scripture quotations marked (TLB) are taken from The Living Bible, Copyright © 1971. Used by permission of Tyndale House Publishers Inc. Wheaton 1L 60189. All rights reserved.

Scripture quotation noted (AMP) are taken from THE AMPLIFIED BIBLE Copyright © 1954, 1958, 1962, 1964, 1965, 1987 by the Lockman Foundation. All rights reserved used by permission. (www.Lockman.org)

Quotations from The Message (TM) copyright © 1993, 1994, 1995, 1996, used by permission of Navpress Publishing Group.

Quotations from the Easy to Read Version (ERV) Copyright © 2006 by World Bible Translation Center. Used by permission.

Quotations from The Voice Version (Voice) The Voice Bible Copyright © 2012 Thomas Nelson, Inc. The Voice™ translation © 2012 Ecclesia Bible Society. All rights reserved. Used by permission.

ISBN 978-09546816-6-1

Forward

"Men who are keen to live out their potential as faithful stewards of God will find this book useful. Rev R C Francis' work is a labour of love. Presented in a simplified way, it draws on insights from his pioneering work with men, spanning over the last 10 years.

As a new study resource, it provides access to a number of useful definitions for men. As a positive contribution to the ongoing conversation on manhood, it invites men to study for themselves what it means to be a man.

The simple step by step layout of the book makes it easily accessible for individual studies. Men studying as a group will also find it beneficial as a discussion aid.

Filled with Scripture references and the meaning of key words from the Hebrew and Greek, referring to men, it equips men to become participators rather than spectators in the conversation.

In the book we are presented with a Biblical understanding of man by Rev Francis that is an encouragement for us to be transformed as men into that Godly image that is in all of us. "It's a Man Thing" is an inspirational book for men to move beyond thinking and talking to acting, in other words to "man up".

Rev Dr Trevor W. Adams
Mentor/Educator/Role Model

Table of Contents

PERSONAL ACKNOWLEDGEMENT

I give thanks to God for the outpouring of inspiration that He gives me on a daily basis.

Since I have accepted Jesus Christ as my personal Lord and Saviour, my life has been transformed.

I know that I have not got there yet, but I strive continually to be the man God has called me to be. Each day I awake I have seen tremendous changes in my life.

Almighty God, my Lord and King, I thank you from the depths of my heart for loving me and caring so much about me. My life has meaning and purpose because of you. I pray that others may come to know your love through your Son Jesus Christ also.

I would also like to thank my beautiful wife Maureen, for her love and unwavering support in my endeavours to write to the glory of God. I appreciate her tireless efforts in editing this book.

Maureen you are a constant encouragement to me and my inspiration. I love you very much. I am blessed to have you as my wife.

To my precious and beautiful daughter Michaela, I love you very much. You continue to bring much joy to your mother and I. May God continually bless your life. I am blessed to have you as my daughter.

DEDICATION

This book is dedicated to: -

- All the men who have attended, been part of, and supported the "*Be That Man*" Men's School of Ministry from its inception 10 years ago.

- All the men that I have counselled, ministered to, prayed for encouraged, supported, and walked alongside with.

- All the men who have been there for me personally in my struggles and times when I was down (you know who you are). Just knowing you were there for me and praying for and with me, made a difference in my life.

- Every man that desires to be a better man, and who have a hunger to be the man that God desires you to be.

INTRODUCTION

1 Corinthians 4:1-2

Let a man so account of us, as of the ministers of Christ, and stewards of the mysteries of God.

[2] Moreover it is required in stewards, that a man be found faithful.

Before we proceed, here are a number of definitions. The aim of this is to cause you the reader to study for yourselves the wonderful word of God.

The word "man" (from the Greek word "anthropos") used in verse 1, refers to all human beings, whether they are male & female (*...let every human being).*

11

The word "minister" (from the Greek word "huperetes") used in verse 1, refers to servants. It means, "anyone who aids another in any work, rendering service".

The word "steward" (from the Greek word "oikonomos") used in verses 1 & 2, refers to, "one to whom the head of the house or proprietor has entrusted the management of his affairs".

The word "man" (verse 2) (from the Greek word "tis" or "tij") refers to "he" or a "certain one" and specifically applies to the male.

The word "faithful" (verse 2) (from the Greek word "pistos") refers to:-

- One who is worthy to be trusted
- One who is reliable

- One who trusts in the promises of God
- One who is convinced, believes, and is sure that Jesus is the Messiah.

Paul reminds us of the following things:

1. That as servants of the Lord we are to remain faithful.
2. Those of us who Minister for Christ are responsible to Him.
3. We are to proclaim the message of the gospel faithfully.
4. Reliability and trustworthiness are some of the necessary virtues for all servants and stewards especially in the things of God.

This indicates that as men we have a responsibility to ensure that the Word of

God is instilled in those who are in our sphere of influence such as our: -

- Wives
- Children
- Nieces and nephews
- God-children
- One another.

We were not made to live like most men live in the world. We were made to strive, to work, prosper, succeed, conquer and give ourselves for something that is eternal.

We are called to advance the KINGDOM OF GOD. Using the giftings GOD has given to us.

God's word defines who we are and what is required of us. It further gives us guidance, direction, and instructions on

14

how to live while we are here on earth, and prepares us for eternity.

Psalm 119:105 Easy-to-Read Version (ERV)
105 Your word is like a lamp that guides my steps, a light that shows the path I should take.

This handy pocket book is packed with clear directives from the word of God that, when studied and applied on a daily basis, will help shape your life in such a powerful way and bring you into a new intimate relationship with God through Jesus Christ.

Enjoy, be blessed, be transformed.

I dare you to **Be That Man**!

PERSONAL NOTES

I AM A MAN

LORD, *what am I?*
I am a man
I am made in your image,
after your likeness.

Who *am I?*
I am me
I am uniquely made
I am special in your eyes
You value me
No one can beat me being me.

What *is my role?*
To function according to your will
to live according to your plan
To allow your word to govern my behaviour

To reflect you in my life in
every way, every day.

What *would I do without you?*
I would malfunction
I am a man, made in your
image,
after your likeness
Made to function according
to your will.

By R C Francis © used by permission

MAN

MAN

Throughout the Scriptures the word "man" is viewed from a number of perspectives, depending on the context that it is mentioned.

Although there are a number of definitions, pertaining to "man" my primary focus at this point is to enable us to come to understand how GOD is central to our existence, and that by being a "man" we can demonstrate and operate in the authority and power of our heavenly Father and manifest all that He is in our daily lives.

I will begin by using six definitions of the word "man", primarily so as not to drag it out too much but to bring out the relevant points needed for this teaching.

The six definitions I have chosen are:-

Hebrew definitions of "man":-

1. Adam
2. Enosh
3. Geber
4. Iysh

Greek Definitions of *man:-*

1. Anthropos
2. Aner

Adam

Definition: Human, earthling, mankind. It denotes man's origin as being from the dust of the ground.

Genesis 1:26 The Voice (VOICE)

God: [26] *Now let Us conceive a new creation—humanity—made in Our image, fashioned according to Our likeness. And let Us grant them authority over all the earth—the fish in the sea and the birds in the sky, the domesticated animals and the small creeping creatures on the earth.*

Genesis 2:7 The Voice (VOICE)
[7] *One day the Eternal God scooped dirt out of the ground, sculpted it into the*

shape we call __human,__ breathed the breath that gives life into the nostrils of the __human__, and the __human__ became a living soul. (Emphasis added)

Genesis 5:1-2 The Voice (VOICE)
5 Here now is the account of Adam's descendants. You remember, when God created humans, He made them in His own likeness.[2] He created them male and female; and after creating them, God put a special blessing on them and named them "humanity."

Additional scripture helps:-

Isaiah 45:12; Deuteronomy 4:32;
Ecclesiastes 7:29; Exodus 33:20;
1 Samuel 16:7; 1 Chronicles 21:13;
1 Chronicles 29:1 (This is not
exhaustive).

Enosh

Definition: Weak or mortal.

Genesis 6:4Authorized (King James) Version (AKJV*)***
*⁴ There were giants in the earth in those days; and also after that, when the sons of God came in unto the daughters of men, and they bare children to them, the same became mighty men which were of old, men (*Mortal Man-Enosh)* of renown.* (Emphasis added)

Psalm 9:19 Authorized (King James) Version (AKJV)
¹⁹Arise, O Lᴏʀᴅ; let not man **(Mere Mortal-Enosh)** *prevail: let the heathen be judged in thy sight.* **(Emphasis added)**

Additional Scriptures:

Psalm 90:3; Isaiah 13:12; Isaiah 51:12-13; Job 10: 4-5

Geber

Definitions: A physically strong or able bodied man; strong man, warrior; strength or ability to fight.

Because an able bodied man depends and trusts in his own strength and physical ability he will be singled out to remind him of the danger of having such an attitude.

Psalm 52:7 Authorized (King James) Version (AKJV)
7 Lo, this is the man (strong man-Geber) that made not God his strength;

26

but trusted in the abundance of his riches, and strengthened himself in his wickedness. (Emphasis added)

Psalm 89:48 Authorized (King James) Version (AKJV*)*

*[48] What man (***strong man, able bodied man-Geber***) is he that liveth, and shall not see death? Shall he deliver his soul from the hand of the grave? Selah.* (Emphasis added)

Jeremiah 17:5Authorized (King James) Version (AKJV)

*[5] Thus saith the L*ORD*; Cursed be the man (***strong man-Geber***) that trusteth in man, (***earthly man-Adam***) and maketh flesh his arm, and whose heart departeth from the L*ORD*.* (Emphasis added)

Additional Scripture helps:-

Exodus 10:11; Exodus 12:37; Job 38:3; Job 40:7; Habakkuk 2:5; Job 14:10; (Geber & Adam); Proverbs 24:5 (Geber & Adam); Jeremiah 17:7

Iysh

When *Iysh* is used its primary thought is man, person, or individual.

It further expresses:- a man of God; a man of understanding; a man of discernment; male; husband; one who is betrothed to be married. It denotes a man, in contrast with a woman, and further denotes a great man, in contrast with ordinary men.

What an extraordinary picture of what it means to be a real man!

When Eve was created, Adam gave her a name and mentioned a connection between his name and hers.

Genesis 1:23 (The Voice)
ADAM: At last, a suitable companion, a perfect partner. Bone from my bones. Flesh from my flesh. I will call this one <u>*woman*</u> *(Ishshah), as an eternal reminder that she was taken out of man (Iysh).* (Emphasis added)

Joshua 14:6 Authorized (King James) Version (AKJV)
[6] Then the children of Judah came unto Joshua in Gilgal: and Caleb the son of Jephunneh the Kenezite said unto him, Thou knowest the thing that the LORD said unto <u>*Moses the man of God*</u>

29

(Iysh) *concerning me and thee in Kadesh-barnea.* (Emphasis added)

Proverbs 10:23 Authorized (King James) Version (AKJV)
*[23] It is as sport to a fool to do mischief: but a <u>man of understanding</u> **(Iysh)** hath wisdom.*(Emphasis added)

1 Samuel 13:14 Authorized (King James) Version (AKJV)
[14] But now thy kingdom shall not continue: the Lord *hath sought him a <u>man after his own heart,</u> **(Iysh)** and the* Lord *hath commanded him to be captain over his people, because thou hast not kept that which the* Lord *commanded thee*. (Emphasis added)

At this point we will take a short pause from *Iysh* to look at two New Testament words for *man* and give a brief overview of how the New Testament relates to the Old Testament in its definition of *man*. After which we will go back to the word *Iysh* to further show how God is central to our existence and that by being a man we can demonstrate and operate in the authority and power of our heavenly Father and manifest all that He is in our daily lives.

PERSONAL NOTES

The NT Man

The NT Man

Whilst this is not exhaustive here are two words mentioned in the NT to define *man*.

a) Greek - Anthropos.
b) Greek - Aner.

Anthropos

a) A man
b) One of the human race
c) A generic term for mankind
d) Men and Women - The Human race

Matthew 4:19 Authorized (King James) Version (AKJV)

¹⁹ And he saith unto them, Follow me, and I will make you fishers of <u>men</u> **(mankind).** (Emphasis added)

Matthew 12:12 Authorized (King James) Version (AKJV)

¹² How much then is <u>a man</u> (human being) better than a sheep? Wherefore it is lawful to do well on the sabbath days. (Emphasis added)

Anthropos relates to both genders (male and female). Both are created in the image of God and invested with individual personhood and destiny.

Galatians 3:28 (Authorized (King James) Version (AKJV)

²⁸ There is neither Jew nor Greek, there is neither bond nor free, there is neither male nor female: for ye are all one in Christ Jesus.

Anthropos answers to the Hebrew word *Adam* which refers to *mankind*, *humankind* and *earthly.*

PERSONAL NOTES

Aner

a) A male human being.

b) A man,

c) A husband.

d) A Gentleman.

1) It is used to distinguish a man from a women.

Acts 8:12Authorized (King James) Version (AKJV)
*[12] But when they believed Philip preaching the things concerning the kingdom of God, and the name of Jesus Christ, they were baptized, both <u>men (Aner)</u> and women.(*Emphasis added)

Acts 17:12Authorized (King James) Version (AKJV)

12 Therefore many of them believed; also of honourable women which were Greeks, and of men, (Aner) not a few.

Emphasis added.

2) It is used in reference to husband.

Matthew 1:16Authorized (King James) Version (AKJV)

*16 and Jacob begat Joseph the husband (Aner) of Mary, of whom was born Jesus, who is called Christ (*Emphasis added)

Other scripture helps:-

John 4:16; Romans 7:2; 1 Corinthians 7:2; 1 Timothy 3:2,12; Titus 1:6

3) It is used in reference to a betrothed or future husband.

Matthew 1:19Living Bible (TLB)
[19] *Then Joseph, <u>her fiancé (Betrothed, Aner),</u>[a] being a man of stern principle,* decided to break the engagement but to do it quietly, as he didn't want to publicly disgrace her.(*Emphasis added)

4) Used with reference to age and to distinguish an adult man from a boy.

Matthew 14:21Authorized (King James) Version (AKJV)
[21] *And they that had eaten were about five thousand <u>men, (Aner)</u> beside women and children.*

Emphasis added.

See also *Matthew 15:38.* [38](And they that did eat were four thousand <u>men,</u> (Aner) beside women and children.)

Aner answers to the Hebrew term *Iysh*, as in male, husband or a man, in contrast to woman.

Now let us return to Iysh.

It is clear throughout scripture that both man and woman *Iysh* & *Ishsha* are created with the same God-like attributes and God-like spiritual qualities.

Man and woman were created differently but with the potential to work in unity toward the same goal. That means they are to give and take, push and pull, share the load, protect and take care of things. Each bring something to the table to unite in glory.

It is also important for us to remember that God gives specific and clear directives to the man and to the woman for the common goal of fulfilling His purpose. Each must work within the parameters of his or her God-given directives to have good success in life and to bring about unity in the home, churches, communities, and nations.

Remember, when *Iysh* is used its primary thought is man, person, or individual.

It further expresses <u>man of God</u>, <u>man of understanding</u>, <u>man of discernment</u>, <u>male</u>, <u>husband</u>, <u>one who is betrothed to be married</u>.

It denotes a *man* in contrast with a *woman*, and further denotes a *great man* in contrast with *ordinary men*.

What an extraordinary picture of what it means to be a real man!

A real man represents fully all that God is. His priority is to do things God's way.

His priority is to fully submit himself to the leadership of God.

When God (or those who flow from God) is spoken of as a man, the word is *Iysh.*

Exodus 15:3 Authorized (King James) Version (AKJV)
³ The LORD is a __man__ (__Iysh__) of war: the LORD is his name. Emphasis added:

Joshua 5:13Authorized (King James) Version (AKJV)
¹³ And it came to pass, when Joshua was by Jericho, that he lifted up his eyes and looked, and, behold, there stood a __man__ (__Iysh__) over against him with his sword drawn in his hand: and Joshua went unto him, and said unto him, Art thou for us, or for our adversaries? (Emphasis added)

Daniel 9:21 Authorized (King James) Version (AKJV)

*[21] yea, whiles I was speaking in prayer, even the <u>man</u> **(Iysh)** Gabriel, whom I had seen in the vision at the beginning, being caused to fly swiftly, touched me about the time of the evening oblation.* (Emphasis added)

Daniel 10:5 Authorized (King James) Version (AKJV)

*[5] then I lifted up mine eyes, and looked, and behold a certain <u>man</u> **(Iysh)** clothed in linen, whose loins were girded with fine gold of Uphaz:* (Emphasis added)

Zechariah 1:8 Authorized (King James) Version (AKJV)

[8] I saw by night, and behold a man **(Iysh)** *riding upon a red horse, and he stood among the myrtle trees that were in the bottom; and behind*

45

him were there red horses, speckled, and white. (Emphasis added)

PERSONAL NOTES

PERSONAL NOTES

Iysh

The Hebrew Word for man is *Iysh* which is spelt *Aleph Yod Shin*, and the Hebrew Word for woman is *Ishshah* which is spelt *Aleph Shin Heh*.

Notice they were both created with *Aleph* and *Shin*. The *Aleph* signifies God's strength and all that He is. *Shin* signifies fire which represents the spirit, tree of life, burning bush and presence of God.

The Hebrew spelling of God is "**YHVH**" which is the Hebrew Word that translates as LORD (capitals) and is used approximately 7000 times in the Bible, more often in the Old Testament.

The title is also referred to as the *tetragrammaton* meaning "The Four Letters".

YHVH also means "to be" "I am" and is the special name that GOD revealed to Moses at the burning bush:-

And God said to Moses, "I Am who I Am." Exodus 3:14-15.

YHVH declares God's absolute being; the source of everything. He is the beginning and the end.

Here is what **YHVH** does. He places the masculine first letter of His Divine name "Yod" (which means *hand*) between the Aleph Shin to make the Hebrew word for man *Iysh* = Aleph **Yod** Shin.

He places the feminine, second letter of His divine name, "Heh" (which means *window*), and places it after Aleph Shin to make the Hebrew word for woman *Ishshah* =Aleph Shin **Heh**.

These additions which define both man and woman represent the Divine Presence. Both share divine origins and attributes but have distinct roles and differences so that together they can become one.

Hand signifies:- **Worship, Strength, Guidance, Work.**

Window signifies:- **Revelation, Breath, Look out**

All of which show God's care for us, love for us and faithfulness to us.

YHVH is central to our existence. We must not ignore God's presence in our lives, or over time we will burn up and self- destruct.

Furthermore, it is important to note that because YHVH is central to our existence, this also shows the oneness of male and female as equal bearers of the image of YHVH and equal status before YHVH.

Each one is equally able to have a direct personal relationship with GOD. **However, within this, God has an order in which we must flow.**

As I said earlier, it is also important for us to remember that God gives specific and clear directives to the **man** and to the **woman** for the common goal of fulfilling His purpose. Each must work within the parameters of his or her God given directives to have good success in life and to bring about unity in the home, churches, communities, and nations.

PERSONAL NOTES

IN HIS IMAGE-AFTER HIS LIKENESS

IN HIS IMAGE-AFTER HIS LIKENESS

Genesis 1:26

King James Version (KJV)

26 And God said, Let us make man in our image, after our likeness: and let them have dominion over the fish of the sea, and over the fowl of the air, and over the cattle, and over all the earth, and over every creeping thing that creepeth upon the earth.

Ephesians 5:1 **Amplified Bible (AMP)**

5 Therefore be imitators of God [copy Him and follow His example], as well-beloved children [imitate their father].

57

The creation of mankind is very significant. It is here that GOD creates a creature that is higher than the animals and a little lower than the angels, which possess a special likeness to Him.

Man is a being that GOD has developed, who is capable of developing a spiritual, functional, and personal relationship with Him. This personal relationship, which spiritually bonds us with GOD, is extremely unique.

Image and likeness complement each other and help us to better define what is meant by the scripture in *Genesis 1:26.*

    a) An image of something is duplicative in nature. For

instance, a statue is made in the image of a person. It also means shade or shadow of something,

b) *Image* describes an exact resemblance, replica, representation, like the son who is the very image of his father.

The phrase, "*making man in our image*", has sparked much debate and discussions among many scholars. But my aim here is to share my thoughts and experience regarding being made in God's image and likeness. I would urge you to study further and ask the Holy Spirit, who only brings the things of God to us, to enlighten you.

I believe that the *image* therefore can be seen as the existence of man as a spirit. It is the equipment that GOD has given us, the capacity to be God-like, not to be God.

The Lord Jesus spoke these words to the women at the well in John **4:24 King James Version (KJV)**

²⁴ God is a Spirit: and they that worship him must worship him in spirit and in truth.

For a spirit hath not flesh and bones, as ye see me have. **Luke 24:39b (KJV)**

A spirit can exist without a body. God is a spirit and I am a spirit dwelling in a body. I have the capacity to be God-like – not to be GOD.

Since I am made from the dust of the ground and received holy breath from God who is a spirit, then any resemblance /replication I have to Him must therefore be spirit. Therefore the image of God in man is the spirit of God.

To be like someone, means that you possess characteristics to that person. It means that you are similar in many ways, in like manner, in the same fashion.

In *Acts 11:26b*

***And the disciples were called Christians first in Antioch.* (Emphasis Added)**

This is because they were doing Christ-like works.

Now remember, **the image** of GOD as we have already seen, is the existence of man as a spirit. It is the utensil that GOD has given us the capacity to be God like. Not to be GOD.

The *likeness* (one who possesses many of the characteristics of a person; similar, in like manner, in the same fashion) *is the proper functioning of that utensil.*

Therefore, when Adam was formed by the creator, he stood before GOD as a spirit which dwelled in a body, exercising the functions of the soul. He had the ability to be creative, to communicate, to relate, and to make moral choices. But he not only had the ability to do so, he was actually doing it. He was exercising the function of godlikeness.

The principle of godlikeness is pushing aside of independence and resting on the working of another who dwells within. **That is what Adam knew. That is the way he functioned,** and therefore fulfilled his manhood and manifested the likeness of GOD.

We must pursue the likeness of GOD.

John 5:19 The Message (MSG)

What the Father Does, the Son Does
[19-20]So Jesus explained himself at length. "I'm telling you this straight. The Son can't independently do a thing, only what he sees the Father doing. What the Father does, the Son does. The Father loves the Son and includes him in everything he is doing.

John 14:10 The Message (MSG)

Don't you believe that I am in the Father and the Father is in me? The words that I speak to you aren't mere words. I don't just make them up on my own. The Father who resides in me crafts each word into a divine act.

Let us read a wonderful verse taken from Colossians 3:9-10 where the Apostle Paul shows us the plan of GOD to counteract the fall of man.

Colossians 3:9-10 Amplified Bible (AMP)

⁹ Do not lie to one another, for you have stripped off the old (unregenerate) self with its evil practices,

¹⁰ And have clothed yourselves with the new [spiritual self], which is [ever in the process of being] renewed and remoulded into [fuller and more perfect [a]knowledge upon] knowledge after the image (the likeness) of Him Who created it.

There is the likeness of GOD being restored in man.

The image of GOD has never been lost, for man still retains the capacity to be godlike. But he no longer operates in His likeness until JESUS is restored in the human heart.

1 John 3:2 Amplified Bible (AMP)

2 Beloved, we are [even here and] now God's children; it is not yet disclosed (made clear) what we shall be [hereafter], but we know that when He comes and is manifested, we shall [[a]as God's children] resemble and be like Him, for we shall see Him [b]just as He [really] is.

Refining like silver:

Malachi 3:2-3Amplified Bible (AMP)

2 But who can endure the day of His coming? And who can stand when He appears? For He is like a refiner's fire and like fullers' soap;

3 He will sit as a refiner and purifier of silver, and He will purify the priests, the sons of Levi, and refine them like gold and silver, that they may offer to the Lord offerings in righteousness.

God is refining us so that He can see His Likeness flowing through our lives again.

PERSONAL NOTES

GOD IS AFTER HIMSELF

GOD IS AFTER HIMSELF

Genesis 1:11-12 King James Version *(KJV)*

[11] And God said, Let the earth bring forth grass, the herb yielding seed, and the fruit tree yielding fruit <u>after his kind,</u> whose seed is in itself, upon the earth: and it was so.

*[12] And the earth brought forth grass, and herb yielding seed <u>after his kind,</u> and the tree yielding fruit, whose seed was in itself, <u>after his kind</u>: and God saw that it was good. (*Emphasis added)

Genesis 1:21, 24-27 King James *Version (KJV) (Emphasis added)*

[21] *And God created great whales, and every living creature that moveth, which the waters brought forth abundantly, <u>after their kind,</u> and every winged fowl <u>after his kind:</u> and God saw that it was good.*

[24] *And God said, Let the earth bring forth the living creature <u>after his kind,</u> cattle, and creeping thing, and beast of the earth <u>after his kind:</u> and it was so.*

[25] *And God made the beast of the earth <u>after his kind,</u> and cattle <u>after their kind,</u> and everything that creepeth* upon *the earth <u>after his kind:</u> and God saw that it was good.*

26 And God said, Let us <u>make man in our image</u> our, <u>after likeness:</u> and let them have dominion over the fish of the sea, and over the fowl of the air, and over the cattle, and over all the earth, and over every creeping thing that creepeth upon the earth.

27 So God created <u>man in his own image, in the image of God created he him;</u> male and female created he them.

Matthew 3:16-17 King James Version (KJV)

16 And Jesus, when he was baptized, went up straightway out of the water: and, lo, the heavens were opened unto him, and he saw the Spirit of God descending like a dove, and lighting upon him:

[17] And lo a voice from heaven, saying, This is my beloved Son, in whom I am well pleased.

The reason why GOD said "this is my beloved Son" was because He saw Himself in His Son.

He wants to see Himself in us.

God is our creator; therefore we have the capacity to create. God is a communicator; therefore we have the capacity to communicate. God is relational; therefore we have the capacity to relate not only with Him but with one another. God is a moral being; therefore we have the capacity to live morally responsible lives. God is love, and in Him is no darkness at all. Therefore we have the capacity to love one another enabling

74

the light of God's glory to shine in all that we do. God is good; therefore we have the capacity to spread goodness wherever we go. God is faithful; therefore we have the capacity to be faithful to God, our spouses, our families, our children, to each other.

PERSONAL NOTES

BIBLICAL IMPERATIVES FOR MEN

Blessed is the Man

Psalm 1: 1 King James Version (KJV)

*1 Blessed is the man (**Iysh**) that walketh not in the counsel of the ungodly, nor standeth in the way of sinners, nor sitteth in the seat of the scornful.* (Emphasis added)

A real man represents fully all that God is. His priority is to do things God's way. His Priority is to fully submit himself to the leadership directives of God.

The man who is blessed, is filled with happiness, joy, and gladness. He acknowledges the favour of God upon his life. He expresses happiness, Joy, and gladness in his speech and actions, and others feel happy and secure around him.

O LORD that you would bless me indeed, that as I follow after you, I can be a blessing to others, In Jesus name Amen.

The word man used here is the Hebrew word *Iysh* which denotes *|man of God, man of understanding, man of discernment, male, husband, one who is betrothed to be married.* This man's manner of life pleases God and refuses the advice of anyone who is hostile to God. He is no longer a servant of sin and he mocks no one.

Prayer:

O LORD GOD, may my manner of life be pleasing in your sight. May I live and walk in the fullness of your intended purpose for me, in Jesus name Amen.

His delight is in the Law of the Lord

Psalm 1: 2 King James Version (KJV)
[2] But his delight is in the law of the LORD; and in his law doth he meditate day and night.

We were not made to live like most men live in the world. We were made to strive, work, prosper, succeed, conquer, and to give ourselves over to something that is eternal.

Real men take great pleasure in, have a strong desire and longing for, and willingly abide in the direction, instruction, teaching, and directives of Yehovah. (YHVH).

This man, studies, ponders, thinks over, focuses on the directions, instructions, teachings, and directives of Yehovah. (YHVH), day and night.

This man does not want to lose sight of not only who GOD is, but how GOD is central to his existence.

Prayer:

O LORD GOD Almighty, I take pleasure in receiving your word. I long for your word on a daily basis. As I receive your directions, instructions, teachings, and directives, give me the strength and ability to study, ponder, think over and focus on them day and night. In Jesus name, Amen.

He shall be like a tree

Psalm 1: 3 King James Version (KJV)

[3] And he shall be like a tree planted by the rivers of water, that bringeth forth his fruit in his season; his leaf also shall not wither; and whatsoever he doeth shall prosper

We are called to advance the KINGDOM OF GOD, by using the gifts GOD has given to us.

God's word defines who we are, and what is required of us. It further gives us guidance, directions, and instructions on how to live while we are here on earth, and further prepares us for eternity.

A real man recognizes that by drinking of the fountain of God's word, not only will he bring forth great fruit but his leaf will not droop, fall, fade, sink, wear away or come to nought. This man also recognizes that by drinking of the fountain of God's word, he will succeed, be profitable, make great progress, and advance in everything he does.

Prayer:

Great and mighty GOD, I acknowledge that standing on your word is advantages and profitable. I therefore choose to be like the tree planted by the rivers of water who brings forth glorious fruit and whose leaf which is connected to you shall not droop, fall, fade, sink, wear away or come to nought. I will make great

progress and succeed in everything I do.
In Jesus name, Amen.

PERSONAL NOTES

WHAT WILL YOU HAVE
ME DO?

What Will You Have Me Do

Acts 9:6 KJV

⁶ And he trembling and astonished said, Lord, what wilt thou have me to do? And the Lord said unto him, Arise, and go into the city, and it shall be told thee what thou must do.

At this juncture, I would like to reiterate this point. GOD gives specific and clear directives to the man and to the woman, for the common goal of fulfilling his/her purpose. Therefore it is important that each work within the parameters of his or her GOD given directives to have good success in life and to bring about unity in the home, churches, communities, nations. and beyond.

"LORD, what will you have me to do", should be the heart cry of every man whose desire is to do things GOD'S way.

As soon as Paul was willing to yield himself, he placed himself in a position where he could hear directly from GOD. He was now at the place where GOD could pour revelation upon revelation into his life and meet all of his needs.

My beloved brothers, the power and ability to overcome, to heal the sick, to cast out devils, to change the world, to be great men, to be great husbands and fathers, to make a difference, is to yield to the plan of GOD.

The place of humility is where GOD wants us to be. We need to be at the place where GOD can come in.

I have discovered that each time I place myself in the Father's hand, and humble myself with a willingness and desire to do things His way, powerful changes take place in my life that I would never have deemed possible. I choose to be the Man GOD has called me to be.

My life is being renewed day by day. I echo what the apostle Paul says in

Philippians 3:13-14Living Bible (TLB)

[13] No, dear brothers, I am still not all I should be, but I am bringing all my energies to bear on this one thing: Forgetting the past and looking forward to what lies ahead,[14] I strain to reach the

end of the race and receive the prize for which God is calling us up to heaven because of what Christ Jesus did for us.

I know that I am not manifesting all of the qualities of manhood yet, but I am taking significant strides to reach those goals.

I truly believe that as you are reading this, GOD through the Holy Spirit is stirring up your heart to obedience. I pray that you begin to take significant strides to reach out and grab a hold of His word right now!

If GOD can have His way with you *right now*, then the ministry He has called you to will begin.

Are you willing to follow HIM, obey HIM, draw near to HIM, and be directed by HIM?

"LORD! WHAT WILL YOU HAVE ME TO DO?"

Answer:

Ephesians 6:10Amplified Bible (AMP)

[10] In conclusion, be strong in the Lord [be empowered through your union with Him]; draw your strength from Him [that strength which His boundless might provides].

MEN! All that is in the Father's house is ours. But we can only receive through obedience, and when our Father can trust us, we will not come behind in any good thing.

The story of the prodigal son (Luke 15), reveals to us how the prodigal son's father had killed the fatted calf and made a feast on his son's return, much to the disgust of his elder son.

Notice the father said to his eldest son: *"you are always with me, and all that is mine is yours" (Verse 31).*

In essence, the eldest son did not realise that he had power and authority to kill the fatted calf at any time.

When we yield and comply to our Heavenly Father, all that is in HIS house is ours.

This means, I can rebuke the devil in JESUS name. I can lay hands on the sick and they recover. I can take control of my thought life and daily struggles and challenges, and so much more.

MEN! We must embrace the divine power and authority that GOD has poured deep into the recesses of our innermost being, then Satan and his cohorts will have no choice but to take more notice of the power and authority which is CHRIST IN US. HALLELUJAH!

Pray this scripture:-

My flesh and my heart may fail, but God is the rock and firm strength of my heart and my portion forever. **(Psalm 73:26 Amplified Bible (AMP).**

PERSONAL NOTES

CLOSING THOUGHT

Psalm 40:4 Amplified Bible (AMP)

[4] Blessed (happy, fortunate, to be envied) is the man who makes the Lord his refuge and trust, and turns not to the proud or to followers of false gods.

The word man when used in this passage of scripture is the Hebrew word "Geber" which refers to a physically strong or able bodied man. and further denotes, strong man, warrior, strength or ability to fight.

Because an able bodied man depends and trusts in his own strength and physical ability he will be pulled up to remind him of the danger of having such an attitude.

This powerful psalm of worship by David, teaches us some very important things (in fact I encourage you to read the whole of Psalm 40). However, I am using verse 4 as a point of reference.

This psalm teaches that our strength, abilities, and a warrior-like instinct, only take us so far when used outside of God's plans and purposes, where self is the focus *(Take Goliath for example - see 1 Samuel chapter 17)*.

However, when a man brings all that he is, all of his skills, abilities, gifts, strength, etc., under subjection to the will of God because he recognizes Him as Creator, and the one who is central to his existence, then GOD will raise him up out of the pit of destruction, set his feet upon a rock and steady his steps. That man will receive a new song of praise in his mouth, and will do everything possible to please GOD and do everything HIS way.

PERSONAL NOTES

I SOUGHT FOR A MAN

I SOUGHT FOR A MAN

"God is looking for Men"

In the times we are living, God is raising up men of prayer, men of integrity, men who are spirit-filled, to bring about a dramatic turnaround in this time of worldwide crises.

The men that God is raising up are those who acknowledge that He alone is central to their existence and realize that through Him they have the power and authority to bridge the gap between sinful man and a righteous God and to intercede for the lost.

I shout out today **"I AM THAT MAN"**.

The Bible tells us in the book of Ezekiel 22:30 that in the midst of a sinful, corrupt and wicked nation, where there was idol worship, shedding of innocent blood, deceitfulness, despising of holy things, profanity, sexual perversion, greed, extortion, uncleanness, false prophets and dishonesty, God sought for a man.

Those things that are mentioned above are pretty much what is going on today.

[30] And I sought for a man (Iysh) among them, that should make up the hedge, and stand in the gap before me for the land, that I should not destroy it: but I found none. (Emphasis added)

The word "sought" which is the Hebrew word "baqash", means, to seek, require, desire and secure.

The word "man" which is the Hebrew word "Iysh", as discussed in the earlier part of the book is, "man", person, or individual. It further expresses a *Man of God. Man of Understanding, Man of Discernment, Male, Husband, One who is betrothed to be married.* It denotes a man in contrast with a woman and further denotes a great man in contrast with ordinary men, and champion.

The word "hedge", which is the Hebrew word "gadar", means fence or wall.

The word "stand" which is the Hebrew word "amad" means, remain, endure, take one's stand, present oneself, continue, persist, be steadfast, stand firm, withstand.

The word "gap" which in the Hebrew word "perets" means, breach, broken wall, bursting forth.

GOD'S desire was, and still is, to seek out and secure a man who will stand out and be prepared to move from a position of being ordinary into the arena of extraordinary. A man who will be a wall of defence and protection. This man will persist in being steadfast and firm by presenting himself in intercession to stand in the breach on behalf of the land.

I shout out today "I AM THAT MAN".

MEN! GOD is raising us up to restore our land, our marriages, our families, our relationships, our communities, churches, nations. He is raising up men who will hunger for Him. He is raising us up to be MEN (Iysh)!

My beloved brothers, let us come in line with what the Word of GOD says:-

Ephesians 6:10-13 Amplified Bible (AMP)

[10] In conclusion, be strong in the Lord [be empowered through your union with Him]; draw your strength from Him [that strength which His boundless might provides].

[11] Put on God's whole armor [the armor of a heavy-armed soldier which God supplies], that you may be able successfully to stand up against [all] the strategies and the deceits of the devil.

[12] For we are not wrestling with flesh and blood [contending only with physical opponents], but against the despotisms, against the powers, against [the master spirits who are] the world rulers of this present darkness, against the spirit

forces of wickedness in the heavenly (supernatural) sphere.

[13] Therefore put on God's complete armor, that you may be able to resist and stand your ground on the evil day [of danger], and, having done all [the crisis demands], to stand [firmly in your place].

Today! I come in line with the call of GOD upon my life. I embrace His Word. I choose to do things GOD'S **way** by putting on the complete outfit He supplies, in JESUS' name. Amen!

DECLARATION

The same GOD who raised up Gideon to stand against Midianite oppression and raised up Moses to deliver His people is the same GOD who raised me up also.

The same GOD who raised up Joshua to bring down the walls of Jericho, and raised up David to bring down Goliath, is the same GOD who raised me up also.

The same GOD who raised up JESUS CHRIST from the dead, is the same GOD who raised me up also.

The same GOD who raised up the disciples, and raised up the apostle among many others, is the same GOD who raised me up also!

PERSONAL NOTES

PERSONAL PRAYER/CONFESSION

I will make the LORD my refuge. In HIM will I trust. I acknowledge GOD as my strength, shield and guide.

I acknowledge today that a real man represents fully all that GOD is. His priority is to do things GOD'S way. His priority is to fully submit himself to the leadership of GOD through the power of the Holy Spirit. I shout out today. I AM THAT MAN.

PERSONAL NOTES

Accepting Jesus as Lord and Saviour

John 3:16-17 Amplified Bible (AMP)

[16] For God so greatly loved and dearly prized the world that He [even] gave up His only begotten ([a]unique) Son, so that whoever believes in (trusts in, clings to, relies on) Him shall not perish (come to destruction, be lost) but have eternal (everlasting) life.

[17] For God did not send the Son into the world in order to judge (to reject, to condemn, to pass sentence on) the world, but that the world might find salvation and be made safe and sound through Him.

114

Romans 10:13 Amplified Bible (AMP)

13 For everyone who calls upon the name of the Lord [invoking Him as Lord] will be saved.(A)

PRAYER

Do you desire to make Jesus Christ your Lord and Saviour, here and now? Then pray this prayer:-

Dear Lord Jesus Christ,

I believe that you are the Son of God and that you died for me. I ask you to be merciful to me and save my soul from all sin. I receive you into my heart and accept you as my Lord and Saviour from this day forward and forever more. Thank you for coming into my life, Lord Jesus, help me to learn of you daily. Amen.

Congratulations! You are now born again. You have made the greatest decision of your life. Praise God!

If you have accepted the Lord Jesus Christ as your Lord and Saviour, or you require personal prayer ministry, or further copies of this book, then please log on to www.btmlifelight.com.

Other books by R.C. Francis:-

Be that Man

Husbands Prayer Booklet

Check our DVD teachings online at www.btmlifelight.com.

PERSONAL NOTES